JUMPSTART
21 Days of Transformation

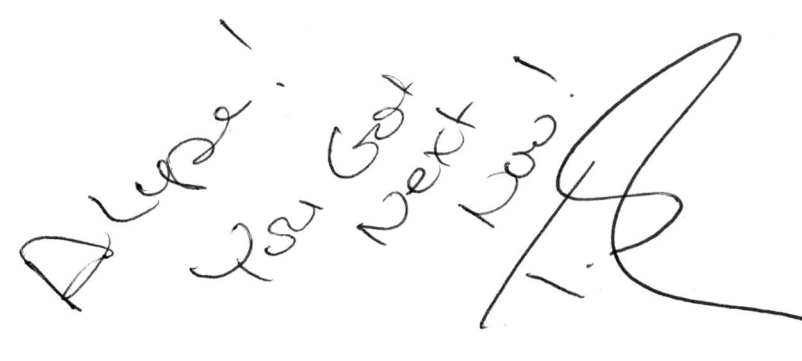

TAWANDA LA'SHUN USHER

Copyright © 2018 by Next Level Beautiful
All rights reserved. No part of this book may be reproduced, scanned, or distributed in any printed or electronic form without permission.
First Edition: March 2018
Printed in the United States of America

Special Acknowledgements

Dr. E.L. Usher, I am extremely grateful to you. Your love, support and understanding have left me speechless. I am excited about what's next! Continue to keep pouring and I will continue to keep pressing forward. From one author to the next, let's continue to write writer!

Coach Sophia Ruffin, you pushed me to keep pushing forward no matter what. Everyday you asked, " Is it finished yet?" The answer is, "Yes, it is finished!" Thank you for being such an amazing friend.

To the Editors:

Ambria McDonald, thank you for your willingness to give of your time and devote endless hours to the editing and regrouping process. I am forever honored.

Jerome Wiltz, you have such a professional touch of excellence with grammar and punctuation.

Kenya Hall, there is such a grace about the way you continued to push. You are amazing!

Traneisha Jones, thank you for such a work of excellence. Your publishing company is second to none.

Natalie Walker, thank you for your edits! May God return unto you what you have given me.

To me family and friends, thank you for your love and support!

Application Brings *Transformation*

This devotional was designed with YOU in mind. Get ready to encounter a daily dose of "Expectation". Isn't it time for you to experience something more than a temporary fix? Your freedom and transformation will come through your dedication to push forward, but you must put in the work that is needed to thrust you into your destiny.

Nothing changes if you are not willing to apply pressure to the areas that need it most. You want to be better in every area of your life, but maybe you're lacking the motivation to bring about that change. You must begin to apply scriptures, write affirmations and set aside a time of consecration daily.

You will begin to immediately see the change within you as you follow the instructions throughout each page. I am excited about your future and I am confident that every word you read will be activated in your life! Isn't it time for you to JumpStart your life to the Next Level?

Welcome to JumpStart: 21 Days of Transformation

Tawanda La'Shun Usher
Author, *Next Level Beautiful: Possessing Beauty Beyond Pain*

Proverbs 18:21 (KJV), "*Death and life are in the power of the tongue: and they that love it shall eat the fruit thereof.*"

Day 1

So many times we have opened up our mouths and destroyed our day. We have spoken words of pain and intensified the pressure that was already present. Anyone can release negative words and change the entire room with unpleasant vibes; but the power comes when you are able to choose your words before you release them. Recently, have you paused and thought about the words that you release before speaking them into the atmosphere?

You have the power to change your atmosphere and your world. Words that hurt and cause pain can delay your move forward. When you become aware of the power that your words have, then will you begin to speak wisely.

Every word that you speak can be either negative or positive.

Your actions and words must match your desired affect. Being positive is a must for your next level. Choosing words of comfort, admiration and love are essential. Understand that when you begin to use positive words, it exemplifies your worth.

It is the season to speak life and not death over your destiny. You have the power inside of your mouth but you must activate it. Remember, your tongue is a powerful weapon and it will kill or bring forth life.

Open your ears and listen to the details of your words. You must realize the very words that you say are the words that will effect your day. When you begin to create an atmosphere of winning words, people around you will notice how pleasant it is to have you around them. And most importantly you will feel amazing being around yourself! That above all, is the highest compliment.

Today, I challenge you to open up your mouth and begin to allow life to flow out of it.

JumpStart Thought:

_____
_____
_____
_____

Affirmation Prayer:

Today, I will surround myself with positive words. Words that will change my future and words that will affect my atmosphere. Assign me to those that I can touch with my words of kindness.

"Nothing matters when you are moving forward."

1 Thessalonians 5:11 (KJV), "Therefore encourage one another and build each other up, just as in fact you are doing."

Day 2

When is the last time you did something for someone with no expectation to receive anything in return? When was the last time you looked for someone else to celebrate?

Today, you will be focused on intentionally building someone's self-esteem. You will not worry about who compliments you. Instead, you will focus on affirming others.

When you encourage someone else, you will feel a major sense of self-accomplishment and appreciation beyond usual joy. Considering others allows you to appreciate them on a greater level. In doing so, you remove your self-absorbent nature and encouraging people around you becomes your mission.

Take a moment and see that someone else is waiting for you to change their day and lift their spirit. Encouragement is not just words, but also thoughts and actions. Often we have waited for someone to encourage and lift us up when it's actually our time to embrace and lift up someone else.

At this moment, someone may be depleted, stressed out, or stretched to their maximum capacity. They are in need of an extra boost and you have been assigned to push them forward. Today, you become selfless and without boundaries! You have been empowered to release compliments to people. Get ready to experience your greatest joy by telling someone else how amazing they are.

JumpStart Thought:

_____
_____
_____
_____

Affirmation Prayer:

Today, I will look for others to compliment and praise. I will remind them of how amazing they are and that their existence matters.

"You have exactly what it takes to win big."

3 John 1:2 (KJV), "Beloved, I wish above all things that you may prosper and be in health, even as your soul prospers."

Day 3

The moment you decide to move forward is the moment you align your heart, spirit and mind to prosper. It is impossible to successfully win in your body with an unhealthy focus. People sometimes label being prosperous as having lots of money, and living a rich lifestyle. They have labeled being successful in material things and flourishing financially as their goal and purpose in life. This is such a misconception. You can have all the wealth and riches in the world, drive the most expensive car, live in the biggest mansion and not be complete.

Wealth is the abundance of valuable resources. In fact, you may be wealthier than you thought you were. Wealth is having stable connections and lifetime commitments. Your positive attitude, the way you handle situations and carry yourself also speaks wealth. Living your best life and taking care of what God has blessed you with expresses your growth and wealth. Your soul being at peace and rest exemplifies true wealth.

God wants you to strive for better and move to a more excellent quality of living. Being prosperous is being progressive! Now is the time to grow and move into your next. Constantly moving forward is your goal and you must be willing to be stretched beyond your norm. Set the tempo to win in all areas of your life: body, mind and spirit.

Living a wealthy life is not only about you, but also about the legacy that you will leave for others to follow. Get ready to expand and explore new opportunities that will not only affect your now, but change your life forever. Everything about your life will begin to flow because you allowed wealth to be more than money. Allow yourself to experience your best life by winning in your health, wealth and soul daily.

JumpStart Thought:

_____
_____
_____
_____

Affirmation Prayer:

Today, I will make better choices for my life because the reward will be great. I will choose my internal wealth as a primary focus for my life.

"Let nothing stop your stride forward."

Romans 12:2, *"And be not conformed to this world: but be ye transformed by the renewing of your mind, that ye may prove what is that good, and acceptable, and perfect will of God."*

Day 7

Today is the day you renew your mind. Your goal is to renew the way you think concerning your destiny. You must imagine a greater plan for your life. How will this transformation take place? It starts by acknowledging and admitting that you have allowed toxic waste (people, actions, and words) to take root in your life. It has entered your dwelling place and caused conflict in your mind.

It is your responsibility to be totally honest with yourself and begin the detox process. Removing the things that have a negative influence and control over your mind must be exposed and released. Any opposing thoughts about who you were in the past and what others have said about you must be removed in order to move forward. God has the power to completely restore the things that were depleted from your childhood to your adulthood. There will be a dramatic change in every area of your life when the transformation process begins.

The question is, "Are you willing and ready for change?" It doesn't matter what everyone else is doing and what their standards for your life are. Many times we want people to like us and want to be accepted so badly that we change and adjust to fit into their perspective of us. It doesn't matter what they think about who you are. What matters most will be the embrace that you make towards your transformation. God wants your mind renewed!

It is imperative that you allow God to release His desires for your life daily. Train yourself to think on things that are lovely, pure, and of a good report (Philippians 4:8). You must constantly remove the thoughts that have trespassed into your space dedicated to God. When those negative thoughts arise, you must pause and practice positive thinking. Once you embrace God's plans for your life and utilize the power of positive thinking, you will gain a peace that will settle and establish you. Be confident in knowing that you will not be consumed by pressure nor will you revert back to your old way of thinking.

JumpStart Thought:

_____
_____
_____
_____

Affirmation Prayer:

Today, I will not be worried about what others think of me or how I perceive myself, but I will walk in the confidence that God has given me. I will push the refresh button and allow my mind to reset. I will embrace the transformation that is taking place within me and walk into my newness that awaits my arrival.

"Everything you experience will impact your future.."

Psalm 120:1 (NIV), "I call on the LORD in my distress, and he answers me."

Day 5

Whenever you are in pursuit of purpose and have decided to turn from your old, many things will begin to arise internally and externally. Regardless of how intentional you are in this season, anxiety will try to come to cripple your peace and immobilize your progress. Anytime you are under extreme anxiety, depression, confusion, or pain, you cannot operate as normal. Your thought process and emotions are compromised. You become unstable and begin to make decisions that are emotional rather than considering the best outcome. Whenever your peace is tampered with, you must analyze your recent circumstances, situations, and interactions. They will help you determine where an open door was created. Make it a point to focus on the things that crept into your space and claimed your peace.

When obstacles come they will cause you to feel overwhelmed. You must not let the things that come to stop and stagnate your progress overtake you. During this time, you must take note of your actions. There are signs that indicate that you are in a dark space, such as words, actions and emotions. You must understand it is normal to have days where you feel overwhelmed and overloaded. In fact, as you press towards your destiny, expect those feelings to increase. They are meant to build your capacity and stretch you for more. You are being prepared to walk in a place of More! More prayer. More provision. More prosperity. More purpose. The problem is presented when you stay there and begin to unpack and get comfortable with that place of distress.

There are a few simple things that you must do to transition from a place of distress into a place of peace. You must first understand that you are not alone and be willing to access the help from the Lord. You must also be willing to immediately change your surroundings. Get up and begin to turn the page. Open up blinds. Get in the car and just drive. Whatever you do, don't remain in that place. Be intentional about moving forward. When you call on the Lord He will answer and rescue you. Cast your cares on the Him because He truly cares about you. He is guaranteed to answer when you call. Jeremiah 33:3 says, "Call upon the Lord and He will answer and He will show you great and mighty things, you know not of."

JumpStart Thought:

_____
_____
_____
_____

Affirmation Prayer:

Today, I call upon the Lord when I am feeling overwhelmed. I will no longer let things overtake my day. Not only do I call on Him, but I have great expectations that He will answer and deliver me from that very low place. He will lift me up.

"The moment you open your mouth, life happens."

Psalm 46:10 (NIV), "Be still and know that I am God."

Day 6

What is keeping you so occupied and busy? What is constantly demanding your attention? It seems as if you cannot find enough hours in a day to accomplish all of the things on your "To-Do" List.

We rush through our mornings to get to our destination without even acknowledging God. Sadly, we continue our tasks of the day and still don't spend time with Him. We seem to be able to fit every new opportunity into our schedule, but still find excuses to not spend time with God. We get so busy with our everyday routines that no matter how much we want to stop the cycle of busyness, something always seems to override our efforts. It would be so much easier to just pull out a sign that says, "Wait until later." However, we start to only make room for Him when situations arise in our life. We start saying, "Lord I will pray every day if you just get me out this situation. God you can have all of my time if you save my family." This is a very dangerous place to be in because we start treating God like a "service." We over promise and under deliver.

It is truly a broken cycle that never ends. We constantly make false promises to spend time with Him, yet He continues to fulfill His promises for us. You must take note of the things that are taking you away from your quiet time with God. You must be careful to not become consumed with distractions. When things are moving around you, God is patiently waiting on you to "be still and know who He is." You must stop and notice that the time you have been given is a gift.
God has given you twenty-four hours to manage but His desire is that you "be still."

When you are still, you have the ability to mentally, spiritually and emotionally rest in Him. Take control of what has tried to conquer and control your thoughts, day and movement. You must begin to put things back in their original order, God first. You will immediately feel His peace and it will carry you throughout your day. Choose to be still and know that God is in control.

JumpStart Thought:

_____
_____
_____
_____

Affirmation Prayer:

Today, I will calm everything around me and listen to the voice of God. I trust Him to lead and guide me into my place of peace. I will not let my busy schedule control every minute of my life. I have the power to rest in Him.

"Don't give up, things are shifting on your behalf."

Philippians 1:6 (ESV), "And I am sure of this, that he who began a good work in you will bring it to completion at the day of Jesus Christ."

Day 7

It is finished! You can rest assure that everything that God has placed on the inside of you is about to be birthed. You may have wondered when will it all happen for you? You may have doubted the process because it seemed as if it was taking too long. Each year has brought you uncertainty because it doesn't look like what you were expecting.

God knows exactly what He is doing when it comes to the plans that He has for your life (Jeremiah 29:11). Why are you worried about the end when you have just begun the process of moving into your season of favor? His Word declares, "What He has started He is able to finish." God guarantees you that He will take action and finish what He started.

God has a reputation for completing everything He has begun. Haven't you checked His track record? Has He failed at anything He's begun? You are a prime example of a completed work. God is not man that He should lie. Therefore, if God has always finished what He has started, be confident that He will complete the plans that he has designed. His perfect will and purpose shall come to pass. You must trust the process and follow His lead because He knows what's best for your life.

You must settle down and watch God work. Do not be anxious and stressed about how it will end. You must remain faithful to see the promise. Be steadfast, unmovable and always abounding in the work of the Lord (I Corinthians 15:58).

JumpStart Thought:

_____
_____
_____

Affirmation Prayer:

Today, I am patient with the process. I trust God fully and know that He has begun a good work within me.

"You have the power to speak life over everything attached to you."

Psalm 139:23-24 *"Search me, O God, and know my heart! Try me and know my thoughts! And see if there be any grievous way in me, and lead me in the way everlasting!"*

Day 8

Daily we should be in a position to allow God to search our hearts. Jeremiah 17:9 says, "The heart is deceitful above all things, and desperately wicked: who can know it?" You cannot allow your heart to lead you. You cannot depend or rely on what your heart says. It is truly possible for you to operate with a broken heart and make unsound decisions based on those issues. Therefore, you are making decisions from a place that is unstable based on what you are feeling and not what you know. A heart examination is needed more often than you know. We allow so many things to come inside of the heart and influence the flow. Life will cause people to walk in and out of your life, and leave you feeling damaged and broken.

Life doesn't stop and wait until your heart is healed. When you are damaged, you naturally go into defense mode by building walls around your heart. A broken heart will reap broken dreams. When these emotional safe guards are in place, you leave no room for anything positive to enter. In order to overcome these emotional safe guards, you must learn how to spiritually guard your heart with the Word of God. The bible tells us to guard our hearts because everything we do flows from it (Proverbs 4:23).

We must ask God to search the depths of our heart. Only He is able to detect, deactivate and dissolve those things that have entered our heart space. Once he reveals what's inside of you, permit Him to destroy that very thing. Once your heart is infused with His love, you will operate on a level of purity. God knows exactly what you need. Allow God to create in you a clean heart so that others will see the beauty of transformation within you.

JumpStart Thought:

_____
_____
_____

Affirmation Prayer:

Today, I will not let my heart take control of my actions. I will allow God to purify my heart and make it clean. I will not operate through a broken heart but ask God for wholeness.

> "Allow the joy of the day to lead you to a place of peace."

Deuteronomy 31:6, *"Be strong and courageous. Do not be afraid or terrified because of them, for the* LORD *your God goes with you; he will never leave you nor forsake you."*

Day 9

Fear has a funny way of showing up when you are right at the edge of your breakthrough. It seems as if all of your hard work, training, and processing over the course of the past few weeks, months, and years have been forgotten, all for something that is bigger and better than your eyes can see right now. Something that wants to keep you from impacting the lives of others. Something that wants to keep you from giving God the glory. Remember, fear only comes during critical and pivotal times in your life to make you afraid to move forward.

When you understand that God is your refuge and your strength nothing can detour or weaken your stride. The road of life can be very challenging, but there is an assurance in knowing that God has promised that He is always with you and will never leave you.

Furthermore, when you are approaching your next level, at times you may feel that you are all alone or that you cannot feel God. During these times, it becomes easy to start moving in your own strength. Be extremely cautious here! Remember, we fall fast when we operate in our own strength. You must trust in Him to lead and guide you. Having unwavering trust in God says, "Despite whatever I may face, I will win because God is with me."

You must declare that your success and strength is in God. Be courageous, be bold, and be not afraid because God is with you.

JumpStart Thought:

_____
_____
_____
_____

Affirmation Prayer:

Today, I will trust the process and know that God is in full control. I will not allow fear to become a factor. I will trust in God to direct my every step. My strength is in God.

"What you say, you shall have!"

John 8:36 (KJV), " Who the Son sets free, is truly free indeed."

Day 10

There is something liberating about letting go of whatever is keeping you hostage. When you get tired of holding on to excess baggage that is keeping you from obtaining your destiny, you will be ready to release it. Freedom is a personal quest that you must seek in order to access your destiny. You have to be willing to throw up your hands and say, "Arrest me Lord, I want to be free!" At that very moment, everything will shift.

When you shift into a position of total surrender, you allow your guards to come down. You begin to feel the lifting of everything that was once weighing you down. Total submission is acknowledging your weaknesses (mentally, spiritually, emotionally and physically) and allowing God to wash those areas.

Imagine yourself running through the rain without the covering or protection of an umbrella or a raincoat with your head and arms lifted towards heaven. When you embrace that moment of surrender, God is able to refresh and strengthen you. God wants everything about you to be free. Your surrender will move you to a place of security and push you forward into your purpose.

JumpStart Thought:

_____
_____
_____

Affirmation Prayer:

Today, I will surrender my will for His will. I will not allow pride to block me from surrendering totally. I am in position to be washed and I am moving forward with every drop of the Father's rain.

"Keep pushing forward, your greatest days are ahead."

Psalm 55:22, "*Cast your cares on the* LORD *and he will sustain you; he will never let the righteous be shaken.*"

Day 11

What are you carrying that is supposed to be cast? What heaviness have you claimed and made a part of your life?

The Bible declares in Psalm 138:8 that the Lord will perfect that which concerns you. Which means God is concerned about what you're concerned about. His desire is for you to lay your burdens at His feet and trust Him to take care of it. Understand that having cares are normal but being overly concerned about those cares can produce stress, worry, anxiety, and fear. You must resist trying to fix things on your own. In fact you cannot fix them by yourself!

How amazing is it for you to have cares that can be cast upon the Lord? Because He is your creator, you must trust Him to know what is best for you. God is not new at fixing problems, it's His specialty. He knows exactly what to do and when to do it. You have to allow yourself to trust the process and believe His Word.

The Lord promises to not only perfect your cares, but to sustain you in the process. God will strengthen and support you mentally by upholding, affirming, and confirming you through it all. Now take a deep breath and cast your cares unto the Lord.

JumpStart Thought:

_____
_____
_____
_____

Affirmation Prayer:

Today, I will intentionally cast my cares on God. I understand that I cannot fix the things that are weighing heavy on me, but I know that God can. I put my total trust in Him.

"Everything that you need is already available to you."

Psalm 46:1, "God is our refuge and strength, an ever-present help in trouble."

Day 12

You give out so much daily! People constantly pull from your time, energy, and even your peace. Have you ever stopped and actually paid attention to all that you do for others? Have you poured out so much that you do not even recognize that you have been mentally, physically, emotionally and spiritually overloaded? Have you been pouring out to others from a depleted place and need to be restored?

Having a place of refuge is critical. It is the place where you find shelter, safety, and peace. It is the place where you are restored and reset. Because the journey that is before you is so important, you must create a place of refuge and demand that no interruptions be allowed. When things rise up against you and you feel as if you have no place to go, that is when you can go to your secret place.

Psalm 46:10 reminds us to be still and know that He is God… You must carve out time daily to be replenished in your place of protection. While there, quiet your emotions and fears; meditate on positive things - things that are lovely and of good rapport; be vulnerable and
allow God to restore you. He is the only one that can restore what you have lost.

God does not sleep and will always be there when you call Him. Rest in knowing that the Lord is an ever present help and finding refuge in Him gives your Spirit a place of peace.

JumpStart Thought:

_____
_____
_____
_____

Affirmation Prayer:

Today, I acknowledge Your presence God. Your guidance will be my compass today and I trust You completely. God you are in total control of my life.

"Focus on what matter's most... moving forward."

Psalm 91:1 (NKJV), " He who dwells in the secret place of the Most High shall abide under the shadow of the Almighty. I will say of the Lord, " He is my refuge and my fortress; my God, in Him I will trust."

Day 13

Do you remember playing "Hide and Go Seek" as a child? Before you played the game, you already knew exactly where you were going to hide. You would run fast to that secret place, making sure you got there before anyone else. There was something special about your hiding place. You felt safe and secure there - as if no one else had access to that spot. Although that was a childhood game you used to play, it has principles that can be applied to your secret meeting place with God.

Where is your hiding place today? What location have you set aside to meet with God? Your Heavenly Father wants you to visit and meet Him there often. Your secret place is bigger than a venue or location. It is an area that only your voice can access and is a place of security, comfort, and peace that has been prepared just for you.

If you do not have a secret place to commune with God, I challenge you today to designate a space. Not only does the secret place allow you to take shelter in God's presence, but it also:

1. Provides you with a space to be transparent. Your secret place allows you to be honest with yourself and naked before God. It is a place where you do not have to be afraid or ashamed. You can just be you.

2. It allows you to obtain physical and spiritual rest. There are times when you just want to hide because you need some alone time. Imagine being exhausted from a long day and the only thing that you desire most is to enter into your secret place,

where you can be comforted and given peace. While there, expect God to fill you up and pour freshness into you.

Remember, as long as you abide in that place He has prepared for you, He will establish you and keep you secure. God has prepared a fortified place of true security and rest. Isn't it time to return to your secret place? You will find that under His shadow is where your strength will be born.

JumpStart Thought:

_____
_____
_____
_____

Affirmation Prayer:

Today, I will focus on abiding in Your presence. I will seek You from my secret place. I declare that peace, security, and rest will be my portion.

"Nothing is impossible when you put your heart and mind into it."

Isaiah 31:19 (KJV), "Behold I will do a new thing: now it shall spring forth; shall ye not know it? I will even make a way in the wilderness, rivers in the desert."

Day 14

Just in case you needed a reminder, your new thing is happening right now! At this very second, you are preparing to experience new beginnings that will thrust you in to your Next Level. You must begin to see yourself in your newness and be ready to experience it. What have you been expecting? What have you been saying? What has been fueling your focus? Do you have projects that have been delayed because you have left them to collect dust?

Behold, God is doing a new thing concerning what is old, but you must be in the right position in order to receive the latest ideas that God is downloading. You may ask, "What is your receiving position?" Your position must be: Facedown. When you are Facedown before the Lord, you are saying, "I am ready for the New!"

While you are face down you will receive instructions on how to proceed with the vision God has given you. He will narrow your focus because He is preparing an entryway into your destiny.

As you prepare to walk into something that you have yet to experience, you may have reservations. Feelings of anxiousness may arise because you are uncertain about the outcome, but the Bible reminds us in Philippians 4:16, "Be anxious for nothing but with everything prayer and supplication, making your request known unto the Lord." Instead, allow excitement, expectation, and anticipation to consume you.

You do not have any time to walk lightly in to your Next Level because it's going to be a *suddenly* that happens in your life. Don't be afraid to spring forth! You will have exactly what it is needed once you get there. God is preparing you for the new. New harvest. New connections. New dreams. New vision. New opportunities. Position yourself to experience and expect the great!

JumpStart Thought:

_____
_____
_____
_____

Affirmation Prayer:

Today, I will intentionally meet you face down. I will not be afraid to embrace the newness that is upon my life, but I will walk boldly in it. I know that you are in full control. I am ready for my New!

"You are blessed and favored by God."

Isaiah 4:31, "They that wait upon the Lord shall renew their strength."

Day 15

Inhale. Now exhale. Feel that? That's your strength being renewed. Life sometimes makes you feel like a superhero. Not because you wear a cape or have supernatural powers, but because of everything you have to balance. You juggle kids, work, a fitness schedule, business meetings and budgeting the bills. You can't afford to miss a beat because if you stop just for a second, everything around you will fall apart. To the outside world you are everyone's hero, but on the inside you are screaming out to be recharged.

How do you get off the merry-go-round? When does the spin cycle stop? What's the fix to the chaos? *Balance.*

There is only one you, and you are valuable which is why so many people and things grab for your attention. Balance is knowing what to focus on and what can wait. Everything is not of high importance. You must know what to choose and how to choose it. To keep balance in your life, consider the following:

- God- Your relationship with Him should be at the top of your list. Set aside regular time for prayer and fellowship. Ask God how to manage those things that cannot be avoided or scratched off your "To-Do" List; and He will show you what is needed to conquer your list with excellence.

- Family- Your loved ones are always top priority. Let them know they are more important than any project that is demanding your time.

- Work- Maintaining your livelihood is essential to building a strong foundation for your family, but remember work has a set amount of time. Work as hard as you can during the time set aside to work. Your integrity and work ethic speak for themselves. At the end of the day, no one will ask how many hours you worked on a project, but they will notice the quality and character of what you produce.

- Self-Care - Set aside time to take care of yourself. Believe it or not, this is highly important. You cannot continue to put yourself last. If you are not at your best, nothing else connected to you will be either.

Life is not a competition, and certainly not a juggling act. There is no prize for completing tasks and accomplishing milestones. When you are well balanced, you are in control of your life; and being in charge of your day will bring excitement and joy to finish each day strong. Inhale. Now exhale. That feeling is a complete sense of accomplishment.

JumpStart Thought:

_____
_____
_____
_____

Affirmation Prayer:

Today, I will not be overwhelmed with things that are unnecessary. I plan to put into action a schedule that I will follow and accomplish. I will prioritize my relationship with God, my family, myself, and my career.

"Trust the process and receive the promise."

Psalms 60:1 (NIV), "Arise, shine, for your light has come, and the glory of the Lord rises upon you."

Day 16

Astronomers warn us to never look directly at the sun because the large amount of light that radiates from it can damage our eyes. This fact is actually unbelievable especially since the sun is located 93 billion miles away from Earth. The truth of the matter is that we still like to look at the sun. We are all drawn to things that shine brightly; there is just something about the glow of the sun; or should it be said, there is something about the glow of the Son!

When you spend time in the presence of the Lord, He will cause His glory to rest upon you. You may be a glory carrier and may not even know it. When you are a glory carrier, there are things that will be attracted to you and will cause you to stand out. Start paying attention to what people say and what happens around you. People will begin to say things like:

"There is something different about you."
"You are glowing."
"Did you change something about yourself?"
"Something feels different about you today!"

The difference that they are referring to is the glory that is resting upon your life. God has highlighted the work that He has done on the inside of you, but the world interprets its as external beauty.

Additionally, when you are a glory carrier, honor and favor are your portion. God causes unusual connections to be made, new opportunities to spring forth, and open doors that were once closed. When the glory of the Lord rests upon your life, there is always provision. Be not alarmed when things start to shift around you and when people start to compliment you. Walk in confidence knowing that God is covering you and embrace everything good that will be released throughout your day. It is truly the glory of the Lord that has come to assist you for the day.

JumpStart Thought:

_____
_____
_____
_____

Affirmation Prayer:

Today, I acknowledge the glory of God that is on my life. I unashamedly glow because of His good works. I will arise to the open doors of favor and walk boldly forward. I am grateful for His presence.

"Get ready to receive major manifestation."

Jeremiah 29:11 (MSG), "I know what I'm doing. I have it all planned out, plans to take care of you, not abandon you, plans to give you the future you hope for."

Day 17

What happens when you write the vision and make it plain, but it seems as if the process is delayed? Anxiety, frustration, fear, doubt, and even desperation all start to show up. The panic of trying to figure it out in the time span that you have designated brings even more stress. The feeling of discomfort begins to drive you to a place of uncertainty, which leads to making decisions that are not part of your destiny, decisions that can detour you from reaching your goals and accomplishing them successfully. You must rest in knowing that God knows exactly what He is doing concerning your future.

You must trust the process and allow God to work the plans that He has assigned for your life. Know that God uses unconventional methods to perfect you. He knows exactly what He has put on the inside of you and what it will take to develop and birth those things out. Understand that in order to achieve those goals that He has placed within your heart, you must activate every gift that He has entrusted you with.

When you totally trust God you will not have to worry about the outcome. For instance, when you approach a chair, there is no question if it is able to hold your weight. You don't ask any questions, you just sit. Literally, you just believe that the chair will uphold you. What more do you expect from the Creator? How do you put your trust totally into something that was made by man? Know that God got this! Instead of getting frustrated with His methods, ask Him how you should navigate and respond. God wants full endorsement concerning Him taking care of you. In other words, relax in knowing that God will not abandon you in the process. You must trust that He will bring those plans to pass.

God knows exactly what He is doing. Isaiah 55:8-9 (MSG) reads, "I don't think the way you think. The way you work isn't the way I work." Sometimes when the process doesn't make sense to you, it makes perfect sense to Him. So, just in case you thought that He was guessing at your future, He is not! In fact, He is very strategic! He already has things mapped out. Even when you cannot see it, God is in complete control. How amazing is that?!

JumpStart Thought:

_____
_____
_____
_____

Affirmation Prayer:

Today, I will not worry or be afraid of the future because I know that God's plans for my life are perfect! Today, I let go and allow God to guide me.

> "Be the amazing person that God has designed you to be."

Psalm 139:14, "I praise you because I am fearfully and wonderfully made; your works are wonderful, I know that full well."

Day 18

It is your season to boldly walk into your total transformation knowing that you are one of a kind. Everything that God created about you was perfectly done. Even the things that you call flaws were beautifully crafted and assigned to you. God's works are unexplainable, unprecedented, and not to be duplicated. Most importantly, when He made you, He broke the mold.

Know that every curve, cut, scar or bruise explains how blessed and beautiful you are. Take a moment and examine the things that make you who you are. It goes far beyond what others can see as your outer appearance. What God has placed on the inside of you is the foundation.

So many times we cover up our inner beauty because of insecurities. You have measured your shape, color, and form by the standards of others. Insecurities will only rob you from reaching your potential. When you understand that God has created with no errors or flaws then you will begin to celebrate His wonderful works. You must allow what's on the inside to exude through you.

Be confident and know that you are such a wonderful work. As you prepare to be the best you possible, start adding fruit to your life. Galatians 5:22 reads, "But the fruit of the Spirit is love, joy, peace, forbearance, kindness, goodness, faithfulness, gentleness and self-control." Inner and outer beauty will be the most fulfilling combination ever!

JumpStart Thought:

_____
_____
_____
_____

Affirmation Prayer:

Today, I know that God has created me well. I will bless Him because I am not living with low self-esteem. I know who He has created me to be.

"Roadblocks will not stop you from reaching your destiny."

Isaiah 41:10 (MSG), "Don't be afraid for I am with you. Don't be discouraged for I am your God. I will strengthen you and help you. I will hold you up with my victorious right hand."

Day 19

There are times when we all have faced some very stressful situations in our lives; the loss of loved ones, loss of employment, severance of business agreements, foreclosure, financial hardship, imprisonment, and maybe even divorce. We wonder how it all happened? Did we miss something? Why didn't anyone block us from the pain that we felt from those experiences? How can we move on from this place of pain?

If you do not take the time to heal from great losses, pain will accumulate. When pain accumulates you become weaker and weaker as time goes on. However, there is victory in knowing that when you are weak, He is strong. You must know that you are not alone. Even though you may be enduring one of the toughest seasons of your life, remember that God sees your pain and will guide you through this.

His love will surround you to build you back up again. It will not be easy putting the pieces back together, but God as your source of strength will help you push through.

Trust the process of your healing and rebuilding stage. Refuse to become discouraged or sidetracked. Understand that there will be some unsettling moments that will come to distract you from your journey. Rest knowing that no matter what comes God is with you.

JumpStart Thought:

_____
_____
_____

Affirmation Prayer:

Today, I will know that God is with me. I will not lose my hope in what I must face, but I will build my faith on what I know. I am pushing forward because God is my refuge.

"There is a blessing in the storm, be strong."

Psalms 116:1 (MSG), "I love God because He listened to me."

Day 20

Have you ever been screaming from the top of your lungs but it felt as if no one could hear you? The issue isn't that people can't hear you. The problem is that you are crying out from a different place that no else can see or feel. The scream that is coming from the inside of you has gotten louder and more aggressive. Is it possible that you have been feeling neglected and now your whisper has become like a thunderstorm? Did someone make you feel so small and so insignificant that you began to silence yourself? Over time, it is possible that unpleasant experiences can lead up to affecting the way you communicate.

It is imperative that once you reach that place of feeling overwhelmed, you must pause and pray. Sometimes we reach this level of exhaustion because we are unable to translate what we are really trying to say. Everyone wants to know that their voice matters and that they are being heard. No one wants to feel as if they are intimated, demeaned, or downsized when they communicate. Also, no one wants to be "over-talked", where they can never get a word in. When we learn to effectively communicate with others, both parties can feel that their words are valued and heard. Effective communication is the art of exchanging mindsets, perspectives, and beliefs.

Being able to effectively communicate is more than talking, it is also learning to listen. Often times, we tend to listen from a place of defense. We are so ready to articulate our points that we don't actually listen to what the other person has to say. What do you think would happen if you allowed others to lead the conversation and you actually listened before you responded? The most amazing thing about God is that He is always ready to listen. Because He truly loves you, His desire is to hear what is on your heart. God does not have office hours, an alarm clock or a rate per hour for you to commune with Him. He is available the moment you access Him. But once you are finished venting and pouring out to Him, you must allow Him the courtesy of responding to you. Just imagine what would happen if you would first approach Him by saying, "I am here to listen to You, Father."

It is time to quiet your talkative spirit and begin to embrace the joy of listening. Get ready to regain your ability to effectively communicate. Not only in how you speak to others, but even in how you listen to God.

JumpStart Thought:
_____
_____
_____
_____

Affirmation Prayer:

Today, I will listen to what God is saying before I interrupt His conversation. I will value those that are speaking and then I will share my personal thoughts. I am honored that God listens to me and loves me inspite of my shortcomings.

"Your greatest manifestation will be jumping forward and not looking back!"

Ezekiel 36:26, "And I will give you a new heart, and a new spirit I will put within you. And I will remove the heart of stone from your flesh and give you a heart of flesh."

Day 21

Today we have shown up ready for open-heart surgery. We are ready to give up the heart that is broke, hurt, damaged and destroyed, but we must exchange our heart for the heart of God. Today, years of unsettling pain, bondage, and brokenness will be loosed. Every chain connecting your heartstrings to the pain of the past will be released. It is time to let God heal your heart.

Pain is unhealthy to carry. It brings physical, mental, emotional and spiritual discomfort. Your spirit must be willing to let go of everything and everybody that has made you bitter, angry, and upset. You must realize that the pain has not helped you move forward, but has only kept you in a place of isolation and restraint. No longer will you reside in the place that is secluded. Truth be told, you have outgrown it.

To be transformed completely you must be willing to go through a metamorphosis (surrendering your old heart for a new one). Just like a caterpillar in a cocoon, you must prepare to be changed into the beautiful butterfly that you are. With every broken chain, you create a crack that breaks the shell of the cocoon around your heart. Every step you take towards purifying your heart of the old, you are moving closer to being free.

It's fast forward form here! You are ready to fly high. Don't you see it? You are such a beautiful butterfly.

JumpStart Thought:

_____
_____
_____
_____

Affirmation Prayer:

Today, I am blessed because I have given up a hard thing. I have released my hard heart. I can no longer return to a place that was not designed for me. I was born to experience freedom.

Made in the USA
Columbia, SC
14 May 2018